The Apostles' Creed
J. I. Packer

Part One:
FATHER, SON,
and SPIRIT
The Apostles' Creed
from *I Want to Be a Christian*

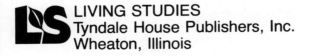
LIVING STUDIES
Tyndale House Publishers, Inc.
Wheaton, Illinois

The Apostles' Creed is adapted from
I Want to Be a Christian by J. I. Packer

Fourth printing, Living Studies edition, February 1986

Library of Congress Catalog Card Number 82-74133
ISBN 0-8423-0051-1
Copyright © 1977 by Tyndale House Publishers, Inc., Wheaton, Illinois
Printed in the United States of America

CONTENTS

INTRODUCTION

The motive that led me to write *I Want to Be a Christian* was to provide a textbook, or perhaps I should rather say, a resource-book, for learner groups, and also a do-it-yourself catechism course for adults who have no access to such a group. From that standpoint, this is a companion piece to my book, *Knowing God* (1972), which has been used widely for group discussion. It offers a series of quick, brief outlines—"sprints"—with questions and Bible passages for further study.

The "sprints," which are written in as compressed and suggestive a way as I can manage, are only pipe-openers, to start you talking and thinking; for anything like a full treatment of each topic, even at catechetical level, readers must go on to the questions and the Bible study.

Catechetical comes from a Greek word meaning "make to hear" and so "instruct," whence also comes *catechism* (the form of instruction), *catechumen* (the person under instruction), *catechumenate* (the organized set-up for giving instruction), and *catechize* (a verb which originally meant "instruct," though the prevalence of question-and-answer methods has given it the latter-day meaning of putting someone through his intellectual paces by interrogation). In Acts 8 we read how Philip instructed the Ethiopian eunuch; catechizing is just that process institutionalized.

Christianity is not instinctive to anyone, nor is it picked up casually without effort. It is a faith that has to be learned, and therefore taught, and so some sort of catechumenate is an essential part of a church's life.

In the first Christian centuries there was a steady stream of adult converts and enquirers, and catechetical instruction took the form of lectures, given at their level. The Reformers' strategy for revitalizing a Christendom that was ignorant of Christianity led them, however, to concentrate on a catechumenate for children. During a century and a half following Luther's pioneer *Little Catechism* of 1529, literally hundreds of catechisms were produced, mostly though not exclusively for the young, some of them official church documents, others the private compositions of individual clergymen. The English Prayer Book catechism, the Heidelberg Catechism, and the Westminster Shorter Catechism are among the best known. Probably most Protestants today associate catechisms and catechizing exclusively with nurturing children, and would not think of presentations like C. S. Lewis's *Mere Christianity,* or Billy Graham's *Peace with God,* or John Stott's *Basic Christianity,* or G. K. Chesterton's *Orthodoxy,* as catechetical, because they are written for adults. But inasmuch as they are intended to instruct outsiders and establish insiders in fundamentals of the faith, catechetical is their proper description.

One great need today is a renewal of the catechumenate for adults. It need not be called that, nor need it take the form of rigid drilling in preset formulae, which is how old-time Protestants catechized children; but somehow or

6

other opportunities for folk in and just outside the churches to examine Christian essentials must be given, because there are so many for whom this is a prime need. Preaching does not help them, for preaching ordinarily assumes in both speaker and hearers confident certainty about the fundamentals of the faith, and where this is lacking sermons are felt to be remote and even irritating because of what appear as their unexamined assumptions. But the proper place for examining, challenging, and testing the intellectual ABCs of Christianity is not the pulpit, but rather the catechumenate — at least, so Christian history suggests.

Modern educational theory sets great store by individual exploration, personal discovery, and group discussion, and there is no reason why today's adult catechumenate should not take this form — indeed, it will be best if it does, provided we remember that Christianity has a given content and continuity, and is not an "x," an undefined quantity, to be re-invented through discussion in each new generation! C. H. Spurgeon's wicked story of the Irishman who, asked how he got on at a Plymouth Brethren meeting, said, "Oh, it was lovely; none of us knew anything, and we all taught each other," has a message for us here. It would be a libel on contemporary Brethrenism, but one has known professedly Christian groups professedly studying Christian fundamentals on which this story would make a very apt comment. Guided study groups on Christian Basics, however, such as some churches known to me run year after year, constitute a genuine and much-needed renewal of the catechumenate, and I do not expect ever to find a church that would not benefit from their introduction.

Biblical quotations, unless otherwise specified, are from the Revised Standard Version. JB is the *Jerusalem Bible,* NEB the *New English Bible,* and Phillips is J. B. Phillips.

I should like to thank the publishers for their constant encouragement, and in particular for help with the questions.

THE APOSTLES' CREED

I believe in God the Father almighty,
maker of heaven and earth;
and in Jesus Christ
his only Son our Lord,
who was conceived by the Holy Ghost,
born of the Virgin Mary,
suffered under Pontius Pilate,
was crucified, dead, and buried:
he descended into hell;
the third day he rose again from the dead;
he ascended into heaven,
and sitteth on the right hand of God the Father almighty;
from thence he shall come to judge the quick and the dead.
I believe in the Holy Ghost;
the holy catholic church;
the communion of saints;
the forgiveness of sins;
the resurrection of the body,
and the life everlasting.

PREFACE

If you are going to travel cross-country on foot, you need a map. Now there are different kinds of maps. One sort is the large-scale relief map, which marks all the paths, bogs, crags, and so on in detail. Since the walker needs the fullest information about his chosen route, he must have a map of that sort. But for choosing between the various ways he might go, he could well learn more, and more quickly, from a small-scale map which left out the detailed geography and just showed him the roads and trails leading most directly from one place to another. Well-prepared walkers have maps of both kinds.

If life is a cross-country journey, then the million-word-long Holy Bible is the large-scale map with everything in it, and the hundred-word Apostles' Creed (so called, not because apostles wrote it—despite later legend, they didn't—but because it teaches apostolic doctrine) is the simplified road map, ignoring much but enabling you to see at a glance the main points of Christian belief. "Creed" means "belief"; Anglicans of former days used to call this Creed "the Belief," and in the second century, when it first appeared, almost as we have it now, it was called the Rule of Faith.

When folk enquire into Christianity, their advisers naturally want to get them studying the Bible and to lead them into personal trust in the living Christ as soon as they can; and rightly so. But as means to both ends, it helps to take them through the Creed, as both a preliminary orientation to the Bible and a preliminary analysis of the convictions on which faith in Christ must rest.

Those convictions are trinitarian. The Creed tells us of Father, Son, and Holy Spirit, so that having found out about them we might find them experientially. The Prayer Book Catechism answers the question, what do you learn from the Creed?—"these Articles of thy Belief"—as follows:

"First, I learn to believe in God the Father, who hath made me, and all the world.

"Secondly, in God the Son, who hath redeemed me, and all mankind.

"Thirdly, in God the Holy Ghost, who sanctifieth me, and all the elect people of God."

When one has learned this much, one is not far from God's kingdom.

"The essence of knowledge is, having it, to apply it." Confucius' formula is nowhere truer than in Christianity, where true knowledge (knowledge of the true God) is precisely knowledge about God—applied. And knowledge about God, for application, is what is offered here, in the studies that follow.

1
I Believe
in God

When people are asked what they believe in, they give, not merely different answers, but different sorts of answers. "I believe in ghosts"—that means, I think ghosts are real. "I believe in socialism"—that means, I think socialist principles are just and beneficial. But what does it mean when Anglican, Lutheran, Presbyterian, Methodist, Roman Catholic, and Orthodox congregations stand and say: "I believe in God"? Far more than when the object of belief is ghosts, or socialism.

I can believe in ghosts without ever hunting one, and in socialism without ever casting my vote. In cases like these, belief is a matter of the intellect only. But the Creed's opening words, "I believe in God," render a Greek phrase coined by the writers of the New Testament, meaning literally: "I *am believing into* God." That is to say, over and above believing certain truths *about* God, I am living in a relation of commitment *to* God in trust and union. When I say "I believe in God," I am professing my conviction that God has invited me to this commitment, and declaring that I have accepted his invitation.

FAITH

The word "faith," which is English for a Greek noun *(pistis)* formed from the verb in the phrase "believe into" *(pisteuo)*, gets the idea of trustful commitment and reliance better than "belief" does. Whereas "belief" suggests bare opinion, "faith," whether in a car, a patent medicine, a protégé, a doctor, a marriage partner, or what have you, is a matter of treating the person or thing as trustworthy and committing yourself accordingly. The same is true of faith in God, and in a more far-reaching way.

It is the offer and demand of the object that determines in each case what a faith-commitment involves. Thus, I show faith in my car by relying on it to get me places, and in my doctor by submitting to his treatment. And I show faith in God by bowing to his claim to rule and manage me; by receiving Jesus Christ, his Son, as my own Lord and Savior; and by relying on his promise to bless me here and hereafter. This is the meaning of response to the offer and demand of the God of the Creed.

Sometimes faith is equated with that awareness of "one above" (or "beyond," or "at the heart of things") which from time to time, through the impact of nature, conscience, great art, being in love, or whatever, touches the hearts of the hardest-boiled. (Whether they take it seriously

14

is another question, but it comes to all—God sees to that.) But Christian faith only begins when we attend to God's self-disclosure in Christ and in Scripture, where we meet him as the Creator who "commands all men everywhere to repent" and to "believe in the name of his Son Jesus Christ . . . as he has commanded us" (Acts 17:30; 1 John 3:23; cf. John 6:28 ff.). Christian faith means hearing, noting, and doing what God says.

DOUBT

I write as if God's revelation in the Bible has self-evident truth and authority, and I think that in the last analysis it has; but I know, as you do, that uncriticized preconceptions and prejudices create problems for us all, and many have deep doubts and perplexities about elements of the biblical message. How do these doubts relate to faith?

Well, what is doubt? It is a state of divided mind—"double-mindedness" is James' concept (James 1:6–8)—and it is found both *within* faith and *without* it. In the former case, it is faith infected, sick, and out of sorts; in the latter, it belongs to a struggle either toward faith or away from a God felt to be invading and making claims one does not want to meet. In C. S. Lewis' spiritual autobiography, *Surprised by Joy*, you can observe both these motivations successively.

In our doubts, we think we are honest, and certainly try to be; but perfect honesty is beyond us in this world, and an unacknowledged unwillingness to take God's word about things, whether from deference to supposed scholarship or fear of ridicule or of deep involvement or from some other motive, often underlies a person's doubt about this or that item of faith. Repeatedly this becomes clear in retrospect, though we could not see it at the time.

How can one help doubters? First, by *explaining* the problem area (for doubts often arise from misunderstanding); second, by *exhibiting* the reasonableness of Christian belief

15

at that point, and the grounds for embracing it (for Christian beliefs, though above reason, are not against it); third, by *exploring* what prompts the doubts (for doubts are never rationally compelling, and hesitations about Christianity usually have more to do with likes and dislikes, hurt feelings, and social, intellectual, and cultural snobbery than the doubters are aware).

PERSONAL

In worship, the Creed is said in unison, but the opening words are "I believe"—not "we": each worshiper speaks for himself. Thus he proclaims his philosophy of life, and at the same time testifies to his happiness: he has come into the hands of the Christian God where he is glad to be, and when he says "I believe," it is an act of praise and thanksgiving on his part. It is in truth a great thing to be able to say the Creed.

FURTHER BIBLE STUDY

Faith in action: Romans 4
                   Hebrews 11
                   Mark 5:25–34

QUESTIONS FOR THOUGHT AND DISCUSSION

What is the essential meaning of "faith" (Greek *pistis*)?

What is the importance of the word "I" in the Creed's opening phrase?

What doubts about Christianity have you had to deal with in yourself and others? Do you think Packer's approach is adequate?

2
The God
I Believe In

What should it mean when we stand in church and say, "I believe in God"? Are we at this point just allying ourselves with Jews, Moslems, Hindus, and others against atheism, and declaring that there is some God as distinct from none? No; we are doing far more than this. We are professing faith in the God of the Creed itself, the Christian God, the Sovereign Creator whose "Christian name," as Karl Barth put it, is Father, Son, and Holy Spirit. If this

17

is not the God in whom we believe, we have no business saying the Creed at all.

IDOLS

We must be clear here. Today's idea is that the great divide is between those who say "I believe in God" in some sense, and those who cannot say it in any sense. Atheism is seen as an enemy, paganism is not, and it is assumed that the difference between one faith and another is quite secondary. But in the Bible the great divide is between those who believe in the Christian God and those who serve idols—"gods," that is, whose images, whether metal or mental, do not square with the self-disclosure of the Creator. One wishes that some who recite "I believe in God" in church each Sunday would see that what they actually mean is "I do *not* believe in God—not this God, anyhow!"

HIS NAME

The Bible tells us that God has revealed himself, establishing his identity, so to speak, by telling us his "name." This "name" appears in three connections.

First, God gave his "proper name," JEHOVAH (or Yahweh, as modern scholars prefer), to Moses at the burning bush (Exodus 3:13 ff.; see also 6:3). The name means "I am who I am," or "I will be what I will be" (RSV, text and margin). It declares God's almightiness: he cannot be hindered from being what he is, and doing what he wills. Well did the AV translators render this name as "the LORD." The Creed echoes this emphasis when it speaks of God the Father *almighty.*

Second, God "proclaimed the name of the LORD" to Moses by delineating his moral character—"a God merciful and gracious, slow to anger, and abounding in steadfast love and faithfulness, keeping steadfast love for thousands, forgiving iniquity . . . but who will by no means clear the guilty . . ." (Exodus 34:5–7). This "name"—you could call it a revealed description—discloses both God's *nature* and his *role*. It is a declaration whose echoes reverberate throughout the Bible (see Exodus 20:5 ff.; Numbers 14:18; 2 Chronicles 30:9; Nehemiah 1:5; 9:17, 32; Psalm 86:5, 15; 103:8–18; 111:4–9; 112:4; 116:5; 145:8 ff., 17, 20; Joel 2:13; Jonah 4:2; Romans 2:2–6), and all God's acts which Scripture records confirm and illustrate its truth. It is noteworthy that when John focuses the two sides of God's character by saying that he is both *light* and *love* (1 John 1:5; 4:8)—not love without righteousness and purity, nor rectitude without kindness and compassion, but holy love, and loving holiness, and each quality to the highest degree— he offers each statement as summarizing what we learn from Jesus about God.

THREE IN ONE

Third, the Son of God told his disciples to baptize "in the name of the Father and of the Son and of the Holy Spirit" (Matthew 28:19). "Name," note, not "names": the three persons together constitute the one God. Here we face the most dizzying and unfathomable truth of all, the truth of the Trinity, to which the three paragraphs of the Creed ("the Father . . . his only Son . . . the Holy Ghost") also bear witness.

What should we make of it? In itself, the divine tri-unity is a mystery, a transcendent fact which passes our understanding. (The same is true of such realities as God's eternity, infinity, omniscience, and providential control of our free actions; indeed, all truths about God exceed our comprehension, more or less.) How the one eternal God is eternally both singular and plural, how Father, Son, and Spirit are personally distinct yet essentially one (so that tritheism, belief in three gods who are not one, and Unitarianism, belief in one God who is not three, are both wrong), is more than we can know, and any attempt to "explain" it—to dispel the mystery by reasoning, as distinct from confessing it from Scripture—is bound to falsify it. Here, as elsewhere, our God is too big for his creatures' little minds.

Yet the historical foundation-facts of Christian faith—a man who was God, praying to his Father and promising that he and his father would send "another Comforter" to continue his divine ministry—and equally the universally experienced facts of Christian devotion—worshiping God the Father above you and knowing the fellowship of God the Son beside you, both through the prompting of God the Holy Spirit within you—point inescapably to God's essential three-in-oneness. So does the cooperative activity of the Three in saving us—the Father planning, the Son procuring, and the Spirit applying redemption. Many Scriptures witness to this: see, for instance, Romans 8:1–17; 2 Corinthians 13:14; Ephesians 1:3–14; 2 Thessalonians 2:13 ff.; 1 Peter 1:2. When the gospel of Christ is analyzed, the truth of the Trinity proves to be its foundation and framework.

It was only through the work of grace which centers on the Incarnation that the one God was seen to be plural. No wonder, then, if those who do not believe in the work of grace doubt the truth of the Trinity too.

But this is the God of the Creed. Is this, now, the God whom we worship? Or have we too fallen victims to idolatry?

FURTHER BIBLE STUDY

God revealed: John 1:1–18

QUESTIONS FOR THOUGHT AND DISCUSSION

What does Packer mean in saying, "But in the Bible the great divide is between those who believe in the Christian God and those who serve idols"? Do you agree or disagree? Why?

What is the basic meaning of God's name JEHOVAH?
What does it tell us about him?

Why did Christ direct his disciples to baptize "in the *name* (singular) of the Father and of the Son and of the Holy Spirit"?

3
The Father Almighty

Anglican worshipers regularly pray the first clause of the Apostles' Creed before they profess it, for *"Almighty and most merciful Father"* is the first congregational utterance in Morning and Evening Prayer. In any service in a Creed-saying denomination it is likely that God's fatherhood will have been celebrated in song before the Creed is said, for it is a theme which with a sure instinct hymnwriters have always highlighted. But how should we understand it?

CREATION

Clearly, when the Creed speaks of "God the Father almighty, maker of heaven and earth," it has in immediate view the fact that we and all things besides depend on God as Creator for our existence, every moment. Now to call creatorship fatherhood is not unscriptural: it echoes in the Old Testament—Malachi 2:10, "Have we not all one father? Has not one God created us?" and in the New Testament—Acts 17:28, where Paul preaching at Athens quotes with approval a Greek poet's statement: *"we are his offspring."* Nonetheless, both these quotations come from passages threatening divine judgment, and Paul's evangelistic sermon at Athens makes it very clear that though the offspring relationship implies an obligation to seek, worship, and obey God, and makes one answerable to him at the end of the day, it does not imply his favor and acceptance where repentance for past sins and faith in Christ are lacking (see the whole speech, verses 22–31).

Some who stress the universal fatherhood of God treat it as implying that all men are and always will be in a state of salvation, but that is not the biblical view. Paul speaks of persons to whom "the word of the cross is folly" as "perishing" (1 Corinthians 1:18), and warns the "impenitent" that "you are storing up wrath for yourself on the day of wrath" (Romans 2:5), however much they are God's offspring.

FATHER AND SON

In fact, when the New Testament speaks of God's fatherhood it is not with reference to creation, but in two further connections. The first is *the inner life of the Godhead.* Within the eternal Trinity is a family relation of Father and Son. On earth, the Son called the One whom he served "my Father" and prayed to him as Abba—the Aramaic equivalent of a respectful Dad.

What this relationship meant Jesus himself declared. On the one hand, the Son loves the Father (John 14:31) and always does what pleases the Father (8:29). He takes no initiatives, depending instead every moment on the Father for a lead (5:19ff., 30), but he is tenacity itself in cleaving to the Father's known will. "My Father . . . not as I will, but as thou wilt . . . thy will be done" (Matthew 26:39, 42). "Shall I not drink the cup which the Father has given me?" (John 18:11).

On the other hand, the Father loves the Son (John 3:35; 5:20) and makes him great by giving him glory and great things to do (5:20–30;10:17ff.; 17:23–26). Giving life and executing judgment are twin tasks which have been wholly committed to him, "that all may honor the Son" (5:23).

God's loving fatherhood of his eternal Son is both the archetype of his gracious relationship with his own redeemed people and the model from which derives the parenthood that God has created in human families. Paul spoke of "the God and Father of our Lord Jesus Christ" as "the Father, from whom every family in heaven and on earth is named" (Ephesians 1:3; 3:14ff.). Human families, by their very constitution, reflect the Father-Son relationship in heaven, and parent-child relationships should express a love that corresponds to the mutual love of Father and Son in the Godhead.

ADOPTION

The second connection in which the New Testament speaks of God as Father has to do with the believing sinner's adoption into the life of God's family. This is a supernatural gift of grace, linked with justification and new birth, given freely by God and received humbly by faith in Jesus Christ as Savior and Lord. "To all who received him [Jesus], who believed in his name, he gave power to become children of God; who were born . . . of God . . ." (John 1:12ff.). The message Jesus sent to his disciples on rising from the dead was: "I am ascending to my Father and your Father, to my God and your God" (John 20:17). As disciples, they belonged to the family; indeed, in that very sentence Jesus called them "my brethren." All whom he has saved are his brothers.

When the Christian says the first clause of the Creed, he will put all this together and confess his Creator as both the Father of his Savior and his own Father through Christ—a Father who now loves him no less than he loves his only begotten Son. That is a marvelous confession to be able to make.

ALMIGHTY

And God the Father is "almighty"—which means that he can and will do all that he intends. What does he intend for his sons? Answer: that they should share. Believers are "heirs of God, and fellow heirs with Christ, provided we suffer with him in order that we may also be glorified with him" (Romans 8:17). Suffer we shall, but we shall not miss the glory: the Father almighty will see to that. Praise his name.

FURTHER BIBLE STUDY

On our adoption in Christ: Ephesians 1:3–14
                          Galatians 4:1–7

QUESTIONS FOR THOUGHT AND DISCUSSION

What does the statement "we are his offspring" say about God's fatherhood? What does it leave out?

How is God's fatherhood seen within the Trinity?

Why can Jesus call Christians his "brethren"?

Romans 8 : 15-17

4
Almighty

The Creed declares faith in God the Father *almighty*. Does the adjective matter? Yes, a great deal. It points to the basic Bible fact that God is the Lord, the King, the omnipotent one who *reigns* over his world. Note the ecstatic joy with which God's sovereign rule is proclaimed and praised in (for instance) Psalm 93, 96, 97, 99:1–5, and 103. Men treat God's sovereignty as a theme for controversy, but in Scripture it is matter for worship.

We need to realize that you cannot rightly understand

God's ways at any point till you see them in the light of his sovereignty. That, no doubt, is why the Creed takes the first opportunity of announcing it. But, though the believing heart warms to it, it is not an easy truth for our minds to grasp, and a number of questions arise.

WHAT GOD CANNOT DO   *God of order + reason*

First, does omnipotence mean that God can do literally anything? No, that is not the meaning. There are many things God cannot do. He cannot do what is self-contradictory or nonsensical, like squaring the circle. Nor (and this is vital) can he act out of character. God has a perfect moral character, and it is not in him to deny it. He cannot be capricious, unloving, random, unjust, or inconsistent. Just as he cannot pardon sin without atonement, because that would not be right, so he cannot fail to be "faithful and just" in forgiving sins that are confessed in faith, and in keeping all the other promises he has made, for failure here would not be right either. Moral instability, vacillation, and unreliability are marks of weakness, not of strength: but God's omnipotence is supreme strength, making it impossible that he should lapse into imperfections of this sort.

The positive way to say this is that though there are things which a holy, rational God is incapable of intending, all that he intends to do he actually does. "Whatever the Lord pleases he does" (Psalm 135:6). As, when he planned to make the world, "he spoke and it came to be" (Psalm 33:9; see Genesis 1), so with each other thing that he wills. With men, "there's many a slip 'twixt cup and lip," but not with him.

HUMAN FREE WILL

Second, is not God's power to fulfill his purposes limited by the free will of man? No. Man's power of spontaneous and responsible choice is a created thing, an aspect of the mystery of created human nature, and God's power to fulfill his purposes is not limited by anything that he has made. Just as he works out his will through the functioning of the physical order, so he works out his will through the functioning of our psychological makeup. In no case is the integrity of the created thing affected, and it is always possible (apart from some miracles) to "explain" what has happened without reference to the rule of God. But in every case God orders the things that come to pass.

So, therefore, without violating the nature of created realities, or reducing man's activity to robot level, God still "accomplishes all things according to the counsel of his will" (Ephesians 1:11).

But surely in that case what we think of as our free will is illusory and unreal? That depends on what you mean. It is certainly illusory to think that our wills are only free if they operate apart from God. But free will in the sense of "free agency," as theologians have defined it—that is, the power of spontaneous, self-determining choice referred to above—is real. As a fact of creation, an aspect of our humanness, it exists, as all created things do, in God. How God sustains it and overrules it without overriding it is his secret; but that he does so is certain, both from our conscious experience of making decisions and acting "of our own free will," and also from Scripture's sobering insistence that we are answerable to God for our actions, just because in the moral sense they really are ours.

EVIL IS MASTERED

Third, does not the existence of evil—moral badness, useless pain, and waste of good—suggest that God the Father is not almighty after all?—for surely he would remove these things if he could? Yes, he would, and he is doing so! Through Christ, bad folk like you and me are

(If we had no free will, God could not judge us.) Must trust God!

already being made good; new pain- and disease-free bod-. ies are on the way, and a reconstructed cosmos with them; and Paul assures us that "the sufferings of this present time are not worth comparing with the glory that is to be revealed to us" (Romans 8:18; cf. 19–23). If God moves more slowly than we wish in clearing evil out of his world and introducing the new order, that, we may be sure, is in order to widen his gracious purpose and include in it more victims of the world's evil than otherwise he could have done. (Study 2 Peter 3:3–10, especially verse 8ff.)

GOOD NEWS

The truth of God's almightiness in creation, providence, and grace is the basis of all our trust, peace, and joy in God, and the safeguard of all our hopes of answered prayer, present protection, and final salvation. It means that neither fate, nor the stars, nor blind chance, nor man's folly, nor Satan's malice controls this world; instead, a morally perfect God runs it, and none can dethrone him or thwart his purposes of love. And if I am Christ's, then—

> *A* sovereign *protector I have,*
>   *Unseen, yet forever at hand,*
> *Unchangeably faithful to save,*
>   Almighty *to rule and command* . . .
> *If thou art my Shield and my Sun*
>   *The night is no darkness to me,*
> *And, fast as my moments roll on,*
>   *They bring me but nearer to thee.*

Good news? Yes, the best ever.

FURTHER BIBLE STUDY

God the overruler: Genesis 50:15–26
                    Psalm 93
                    Acts 4:23–31

QUESTIONS FOR THOUGHT AND DISCUSSION

What does "almighty" mean? Why is it important to believe that God is almighty?

In what sense, if any, is it true to say that there are some things which even omnipotence cannot do?

Is God's power limited by man's free will? Why or why not?

Evil: Consequence of mans free-will, Disobedience to God.

Christian Faith is a _relationship_.

5
Maker of
Heaven and Earth

"In the beginning God created the heavens and the earth"; so begins the Bible. ("Heavens and earth" is Bible language for "everything that is.")

It is arguable how much (or how little) Genesis 1 and 2 tell us about the *method* of creation—whether, for instance, they do or do not rule out the idea of physical organisms evolving through epochs of thousands of years. What is clear, however, is that their main aim is to tell us not how the world was made, but who made it.

INTRODUCING THE ARTIST

The solution-chapter in one of Dorothy Sayers' detective stories is called "When You Know How You Know Who." Genesis 1 and 2, however, tell us *who* without giving many answers about *how*. Some today may think this a defect; but in the long perspective of history our present-day "scientific" preoccupation with *how* rather than *who* looks very odd in itself. Rather than criticize these chapters for not feeding our secular interest, we should take from them needed rebuke of our perverse passion for knowing Nature without regard for what matters most; namely, knowing Nature's Creator.

The message of these two chapters is this: "You have seen the sea? the sky? sun, moon and stars? You have watched the birds and the fish? You have observed the landscape, the vegetation, the animals, the insects, all the big things and little things together? You have marveled at the wonderful complexity of human beings, with all their powers and skills, and the deep feelings of fascination, attraction, and affection that men and women arouse in each other? Fantastic, isn't it? Well now, meet the one who is behind it all!" As if to say: now that you have enjoyed these works of art, you must shake hands with the artist; since you were thrilled by the music, we will introduce you to the composer. It was to show us the Creator rather than the creation, and to teach us knowledge of God rather than physical science, that Genesis 1 and 2, along with such celebrations of creation as Psalm 104 and Job 38–41, were written.

In creating, God was craftsman and more. Craftsmen shape existing material, and are limited by it, but no material existed at all till God said "Let there be . . ." To make this point theologians speak of creation "out of nothing," meaning *not* that nothing was a sort of a something(!) but that God in creating was absolutely free and unrestricted, and that nothing determined or shaped what he brought into being save his own idea of what he would like.

CREATOR AND CREATURE

The Creator-creature distinction is basic to the Bible view of God's lordship in providence and grace, and indeed to all true thought about God and man. That is why it is in the Creed. Its importance is at least threefold.

First, *it stops misunderstanding of God.* God made us in his image, but we tend to think of him in ours! ("Man made God in his own image" was a crack by Voltaire, rather too true to be good.) But the Creator-creature distinction reminds us that God does not depend on us as we depend on him, nor does he exist by our will and for our pleasure, nor may we think of his personal life as being just like ours. As creatures we are limited; we cannot know everything at once, nor be present everywhere, nor do all we should like to do, nor continue unchanged through the years. But the Creator is not limited in these ways. Therefore we find him *incomprehensible*—by which I mean, not *making no sense,* but *exceeding our grasp.* We can no more take his measure than our dogs and cats can take our measure. When Luther told Erasmus that his thoughts of God were *too human,* he was uprooting in principle all the rationalistic religion that has ever infected the church—and rightly too! We must learn to be self-critical in our thinking about God.

Second, *this distinction stops misunderstanding of the world.* The world exists in its present stable state by the will and power of its Maker. Since it is his world, we are not its owners, free to do as we like with it, but its stewards, answerable to him for the way we handle its resources. And since it is his world, we must not depreciate it. Much religion has built on the idea that the material order—reality as experienced through the body, along with the body that experiences it—is evil, and therefore to be refused and ignored as far as possible. This view, which dehumanizes its devotees, has sometimes called itself Christian, but it is really as un-Christian as can be. For matter, being made by God, was and is *good* in his eyes (Genesis 1:31), and so should be so in ours (1 Timothy 4:4). We serve God by using and enjoying temporal things gratefully, with a sense of their value to him, their Maker, and of his generosity in giving them to us. It is an ungodly and, indeed, inhuman super-spirituality which seeks to serve the Creator by depreciating any part of his creation.

Third, *this distinction stops misunderstanding of ourselves.* As man is not his own maker, so he may not think of himself as his own master. "God made me for himself, to serve him here." God's claim upon us is the first fact of life that we must face, and we need a healthy sense of our creaturehood to keep us facing it.

FURTHER BIBLE STUDY

God the Creator: Genesis 1, 2
Isaiah 45:9–25

QUESTIONS FOR THOUGHT AND DISCUSSION

What is the significance of God's words "Let there be. . ."?

What does the "Creator-creature distinction" which Packer discusses have to do with God making man in his own image?

Why can we say with confidence that the material order is not evil?

6

And in Jesus Christ

"I believe in God the Father . . . and in Jesus Christ his only Son our Lord." So the Creed declares. When it called God "maker of heaven and earth," it parted company with Hinduism and Eastern faiths generally; now, by calling Jesus Christ God's only Son, it parts company with Judaism and Islam and stands quite alone. This claim for Jesus is both the touchstone of Christianity and the ingredient that makes it unique. As the whole New Testament was written to make and justify the claim, we should

35

not be surprised when we find the Creed stating it with fuller detail than it states anything else.

CHRIST AT THE CENTER

This claim is central to the layout of the Creed, for the long section on Jesus Christ stands between the two shorter sections on the Father and the Spirit. And it is central to the faith of the Creed, for we could not know about the Trinity, or salvation, or resurrection and life everlasting, apart from Jesus Christ. It was Jesus Christ, in his redemption of all God's people, who was the revealer of all these truths.

See how the Creed presents him.

Jesus (Greek for Joshua, meaning "God is Savior") is his proper name. It identifies him as a historical person, Mary's son from Nazareth in Galilee, a Jewish ex-carpenter who worked for three years as a rural rabbi and was put to death by the Roman authorities about A.D. 30. The four Gospels describe his ministry in some detail.

Christ (literally, "the anointed one") is not a surname, except in the old sense in which surnames like Smith, Taylor, Packer, or Clark declared a man's trade or profession. "Christ" is what Presbyterians would call an "office-title," identifying Jesus as God's appointed savior-king for whom the Jews had long been waiting. Since the Christ was expected to set up God's reign and be hailed as overlord throughout the world, to call Jesus *Christ* was to claim for him a decisive place in history and a universal dominion which all men everywhere must acknowledge. The first Christians did this quite self-consciously; one sees them doing it in the speeches recorded in Acts (see 2:22–36; 3:12–26; 5:29–32; 10:34–43; 13:26–41; etc.). "To this end Christ died and lived again, that he might be Lord both of the dead and of the living" (Romans 14:9). "At the name of Jesus every knee should bow" (Philippians 2:10).

Also, the title *Christ* expresses the claim that Jesus fulfilled all three ministries for which men were anointed in Old Testament times, being *prophet* (a messenger from God) and *priest* (one who mediates with God for us by sacrifice) as well as being *king.*

The glory of this conjunction of roles is only seen when we relate it to our actual needs. What do we sinners need for a right and good relationship with God? First, we are ignorant of him and need instruction—for no satisfying relationship is possible with a person about whom you know little or nothing. Second, we are estranged from him and need reconciliation—otherwise we shall end up unaccepted, unforgiven, and unblessed, strangers to his fatherly love and exiles from the inheritance which is in store for those who are his children. Third, we are weak, blind, and foolish when it comes to the business of living for God, and we need someone to guide, protect, and strengthen us—which is how the regal role was understood in Old Testament Israel. Now in the person and ministry of the one man, Jesus Christ, this threefold need is completely and perfectly met! Hallelujah!

> *Great Prophet of my God!*
> *My tongue would bless thy name;*
> *By thee the joyful news*
> *Of our salvation came;*
> *The joyful news of sins forgiven,*
> *Of hell subdued, and peace with heaven.*
>
> *Jesus, my great High Priest,*
> *Offered his blood and died;*
> *My guilty conscience seeks*
> *No sacrifice beside;*
> *His powerful blood did once atone,*
> *And now it pleads before the throne.*
>
> *My dear Almighty Lord,*
> *My conqueror and my King,*

Thy sceptre, and thy sword,
  Thy reigning grace I sing.
Thine is the power; behold, I sit
In willing bonds before thy feet.

THE DIVINE LORD

Jesus, who is the Christ (says the Creed), is God's *only Son.* This identifies Mary's boy as the second person of the eternal Trinity, the Word who was the Father's agent in making the world and sustaining it right up to the present (John 1:1–14; Colossians 1:13–20; Hebrews 1:1–3). Staggering? Yes, certainly, but this identification is the heart of Christianity. "The word of God became a human being and lived among us" (John 1:14, Phillips).

"Our Lord" follows straight from this. If Jesus is God the Son, our co-creator, and is also Christ, the anointed savior-king, now risen from death and reigning (sitting, as the Creed puts it, "on the right hand of God the Father almighty," in the place of authority and power), then he has a right to rule us, and we have no right to resist his claim. As he invaded space and time in Palestine nearly 2,000 years ago, so he invades our personal space and time today, with the same purpose of love that first brought him to earth. "Come, follow me" was his word then, and it is so still.

Is he, then, your Lord? For all who say the Creed, this question is inescapable; for how can you say "our Lord" in church till you have first said "my Lord" in your heart?

FURTHER BIBLE STUDY

Jesus—God and man: Hebrews 1:1—3:6

QUESTIONS FOR THOUGHT AND DISCUSSION

What is the significance, historically and for us today, of the name "Jesus"?

38

What should the title "Christ" have meant to a waiting Jewish nation? What should it mean to us?

Why can Christ rightfully claim authority to rule your life?

Jesus - "Joshua"; God is Savior;
    historical personage

Christ - Messiah (Gr. equiv.)
    "Anointed One"

Lord - title, authority, uncontested
    ruler/master

Son - God decreed, equal w/God,
    relationship identifier

John 1:12
Romans 8:12-17

[handwritten notes at top of page:]

John 1:14 ⎫ One + only son
John 3:16 ⎬ vs
1 John 4:9 ⎭ only begotten son

"Monogenes" greek word
(not birth or offspring)
To come forth from; of
the same kind, origin, stock.
[Only Jesus is this kind
of Son.]

7

His
Only Son

When you hear a young man introduced as "my only son" you know he is the apple of his father's eye. The words reveal affection. When the Creed calls Jesus God's "only Son" (echoing "only begotten" in John 1:18; 3:16, 18) the implication is the same. Jesus, as God's only Son, enjoys his Father's dearest love. God said so himself when speaking from heaven to identify Jesus at his baptism and transfiguration: "This is my beloved Son . . ." (Matthew 3:17; 17:5).

40

FULLY GOD

Moreover, this phrase of the Creed is a bulwark against such lowering and denial of Jesus' deity as one finds in Unitarianism and the cults. Jesus was not just a God-inspired good man: nor was he a super-angel, first and finest of all creatures, called "god" by courtesy because he is far above men (which is what Arians said in the fourth century, and Jehovah's Witnesses say today). Jesus was, and remains, God's only Son, as truly and fully God as his Father is. God's will, said Jesus, is that "all may honor the Son, even as they honor the Father" (John 5:23), a statement which knocks Unitarianism flat.

But is it not mere mythology to talk of a Father-Son relationship within the Godhead? No; for Jesus himself talked this way. He called God "my Father," and himself (not *"a"* but) *"the* Son." He spoke of a unique and eternal Father-Son relation, into which he had come to bring others. "No one knows the Father except the Son and any one to whom the Son chooses to reveal him" (Matthew 11:27).

BEGOTTEN

"Begotten of his Father before all worlds . . . begotten, not made," says the Nicene Creed. This is the language of fourth-century debate. The point of it is that though the Son lives his life in dependence on the Father, because that is his nature ("I live because of the Father," John 6:57), he is in himself divine and eternal, and is not a created being. The phrase is not suggesting that the Son originated after the Father, or is in himself less than the Father.

"Begotten" in John's adjective "only begotten" cannot signify an event in God's past which is not also part of his present, since it is only for us creatures who live in time that momentary events exist. Time as we know it is part of creation, and its Maker is not subject to its limita-

41

tions, any more than he is subject to the limitations of created space. For us, life is a sequence of moments, and future and past events (begettings, or any other) are both out of reach; but to God (so we must suppose, though we cannot imagine it) all events are constantly present in an eternal Now.

So the pre-mundane "begetting" of the Son (as distinct from the temporal and metaphorical "begetting" of the king in Psalm 2:7, which is applied to Christ in Acts 13:33 and Hebrews 1:5, 5:5, and which means simply bringing him to the throne) must be thought of not as a momentary event whereby God, after being singular, became plural, but as an eternal relationship whereby the first person is always Father to the Son and the second is always Son to the Father. In the third century Origen happily expressed this thought by speaking of the "eternal generation" of the Son. It is part of the unique glory of the triune God.

MYSTERY

Formulae for the incarnation—the Council of Chalcedon's "one person in two natures, fully God and fully man," or Karl Barth's "God for man, and man for God"—sound simple, but the thing itself is unfathomable. It is easy to shoot down the ancient heresies that the Son took a human body without a human soul, or that he was always two persons under one skin, and with them the modern heresy that the "enfleshing" of the Son was merely a special case of the indwelling of the Spirit, so that Jesus was not God, but merely a God-filled man—but to grasp what the incarnation was in positive terms is beyond us. Don't worry, though; you do not need to know how God became man in order to know Christ! Understand it or not, the fact remains that "the Word became flesh" (John 1:14); it was the supreme, mind-blowing miracle; love prompted it; and our part is not to speculate about it and scale it down,

but to wonder and adore and love and exalt "Jesus Christ
. . . the same yesterday and today and for ever" (Hebrews
13:8).

> *Answer thy mercy's whole design,*
> *My God incarnated for me;*
> *My spirit make thy radiant shrine,*
> *My light and full salvation be;*
> *And through the shades of death unknown*
> *Conduct me to thy dazzling throne.*

FURTHER BIBLE STUDY

God's incarnate Son: Colossians 1:13–23

QUESTIONS FOR THOUGHT AND DISCUSSION

Why is it not enough to call Jesus God-inspired, a supe-
rior angel, or even a god?

What is the significance of the fact that the Son is not
a created being?

Why does facing Christianity mean facing up to Jesus
Christ?

Try to explain it

8
Born of the
Virgin Mary

The Bible says that the Son of God entered and left this world by acts of supernatural power. His exit was by resurrection-plus-ascension, and his entry by virgin birth: both fulfilling Old Testament anticipations (see Isaiah 7:14 for the virgin birth, and 53:10–12 for resurrection-ascension).

The entry and exit miracles carry the same message. First, they confirm that Jesus, though not less than man, was more than man. His earthly life, though fully human, was also divine. He, the co-creator, was in this world—his own world—as a visitor; he came from God, and went to God.

The Fathers appealed to the virgin birth as proof, not that Jesus was truly divine as distinct from being merely human, but that he was truly human as distinct from merely looking human as ghosts and angels might do, and it was probably as a witness against *docetism* (as this view was called) that the virgin birth was included in the Creed. But it witnesses against *humanitarianism* (the view that Jesus was just a fine man) with equal force.

Second, these two miracles indicate Jesus' freedom from sin. Virgin-born, he did not inherit the guilty twist called original sin: his manhood was untainted, and his acts, attitudes, motives, and desires were consequently faultless. The New Testament emphasizes his sinlessness (see John 8:29, 46; Romans 5:18ff.; 2 Corinthians 5:21; Hebrews 4:15; 7:26; 1 Peter 2:22–24; etc.). Being sinless, he could not be held by death once his sacrifice was done.

TWO STORIES

The New Testament gives two complementary accounts of the virgin birth, evidently independent yet strikingly harmonious—Joseph's story in Matthew 1 and Mary's in Luke 1, 2. Both show every sign of being sober history. Ancient historians, seeing themselves as artists and moralists, usually omitted reference to sources, but Luke drops a broad hint that he had had Mary's narrative firsthand (cf. 2:51 with 1:1–3).

Matthew and Luke give two genealogies of Jesus (Matthew 1:2–17; Luke 3:23–38), which has puzzled some, but there are at least two straightforward ways of harmonizing them. Either Luke's genealogy gives Mary's line, but starts with Joseph as Jesus' putative father (verse 23) because it was standard practice to declare descent through males, or else Luke traces Joseph's biological descent as distinct from the royal line of succession which Matthew appears to follow throughout. (See Prof. F. F. Bruce, "Genealogy of Jesus Christ," in *The New Bible Dictionary* for the details.)

SKEPTICISM

For the past century and a half skepticism about both Jesus' virgin birth and his physical resurrection has been quite unreasonably strong. It began as part of a rationalistic quest for a non-miraculous Christianity, and though that quest is now out of fashion (and a good thing too) the skepticism lingers on, clinging to the minds of Christian people as the smell of cigarettes clings to the room after the ashtrays have been cleared. It is no doubt possible (though it is neither easy nor natural) to believe in the incarnation of the eternal, pre-existing Son while disbelieving the entry and exit miracles; greater inconsistencies have been known; but it is much more logical, indeed the only reasonable course, to hold that since on other grounds we acknowledge Jesus as the Word made flesh, these two miracles, as elements in the larger miracle of the Son's incarnate life, raise no special difficulty.

Certainly, if we deny the virgin birth because it was a miracle, we should in logic deny Jesus' bodily resurrection too. These miracles are on a par, and it is unreasonable to accept either while rejecting the other.

Mary was a virgin till after Jesus' birth, but later ideas of her perpetual virginity are merely fanciful. The Gospels show that Jesus had brothers and sisters (Mark 3:31; 6:3).

"Conceived by the Holy Ghost, born of the Virgin Mary" in the Creed witnesses to the reality of the Incarnation, not the glory of Jesus' mother: the Roman Catholic Church, however, has sponsored the unhappy development of Mariology (Mary-doctrine) among theologians and Mariolatry (Mary-worship) among the faithful. Mariology which sees Mary as co-redeemer rests on the nonbiblical teaching that Mary, like Jesus, was born without sin (the immaculate conception) and entered resurrection glory straight after death (the assumption).

But the real Mary, the Mary of Scripture, saw herself simply as a saved sinner. "My spirit hath rejoiced in God my Saviour" (Luke 1:47, KJV). She sets us a marvelous example, not just of the privilege (and the price!) of cooperating in God's plan to bless the world (see Luke 1:38; 2:35), but also of humble response to God's grace. Parents are slow to take things from their children, and Jesus himself commented sadly at one stage that "a prophet is not without honor except . . . in his own house" (Matthew 13:57); but Mary and her family, after initial disbelief (cf. Matthew 13:57; Mark 3:20ff., 31–35; John 7:3–5), came to living faith in her son (Acts 1:14). Have we learned from their example?

FURTHER BIBLE STUDY

The virgin birth: Matthew 1:1–25
Luke 1:26–56

QUESTIONS FOR THOUGHT AND DISCUSSION

What do the miracles associated with Christ's earthly entry and exit show us about him?

Do you agree that one's attitude toward the virgin birth and the resurrection of Jesus should be the same?

How does the biblical picture of Mary compare with that traditionally given by the Roman Catholic Church?

9
Suffered
under Pontius Pilate

Fancy a school of scientists or philosophers, or the members of a political party, constantly repeating that their founder was put to death by the government, as a threat to law and order! Yet this is what Christians do, and the cross of Jesus is the centerpiece of the Creed. "Suffered under Pontius Pilate, was crucified." Look at these words in reverse order.

"Was crucified." This was the standard Roman way of

executing criminals. To say "Jesus was crucified" is like saying he was hanged, or went to the electric chair.

PILATE

"Under Pontius Pilate." Hitler will be remembered as the man who gassed the Jews, and Pilate, a nonentity otherwise, goes down in history as the man who killed Jesus. Under the Roman occupation, the Jewish authorities could not execute anyone, so when they had passed sentence on Jesus for confessing his true identity as God's savior-king, the Christ (they thought the confession blasphemous), they passed him on to the governor for action.

Pilate, having symbolically washed his hands of the matter—the goofiest gesture, perhaps, of all time—gave the green light for judicial murder, directing that Jesus, though guiltless, should die all the same to keep people happy. Pilate saw this as shrewd government; how cynical can you get?

PASSION

"Suffered." This word carries not only the everyday meaning of bearing pain, but also the older and wider sense of being the object affected by someone else's action. The Latin is *passus*, whence the noun "passion." Both God and men were agents of Jesus' passion: "this Jesus, delivered up according to the plan and foreknowledge of God, you crucified and killed by the hands of lawless men" (Acts 2:23, from Peter's first sermon). God's purpose at the cross was as real as was the guilt of the crucifiers.

What was God's purpose? Judgment on sin, for the sake of mercy to sinners. The miscarrying of human justice was the doing of divine justice. Jesus knew on the cross all the pain, physical and mental, that man could inflict and also the divine wrath and rejection that my sins deserve; for he was there in my place, making atonement for me. "All we like sheep have gone astray . . . and the Lord has laid on him the iniquity of us all" (Isaiah 53:6).

> Because the sinless Saviour died
> My sinful soul is counted free;
> For God, the Just, is satisfied
> To look on him—and pardon me.

PROPITIATION

Here we reach the real heart—the heart of the heart, we may say—of Christianity; for if the incarnation is its shrine, the Atonement is certainly its holy of holies. If the incarnation was the supreme miracle, it was yet only the first of a series of steps down from the joy and bliss of heaven to the pain and shame of Calvary (Philippians 2:5–8). The reason why the Son of God became man was to shed his blood as (in the Prayer Book's words) "a full, perfect, and sufficient sacrifice, oblation, and satisfaction, for the sins of the whole world." God "did not spare his own Son, but gave him up for us all" (Romans 8:32): that was the measure of his love (cf. 5:5–8).

It is in the same terms—terms, that is, not of tolerant avuncular benevolence, but of this particular precious gift —that John explains what he means by his great and glorious, but much-misunderstood, declaration, *"God is love."* "In this is love," he explains, "not that we loved God but that [when we didn't] he loved us and sent his Son to be the expiation [better, propitiation] for our sins" (1 John 4:8–10).

The cross of Christ has many facets of meaning. As our sacrifice for sins, it was *propitiation* (Romans 3:25; 1 John 2:2; 4:10; cf. Hebrews 2:17); that is, a means of quenching God's personal penal wrath against us by blotting out our sins from his sight. ("Expiation" in the RSV rendering of these texts signifies only "a means of blotting out sins," which is an inadequate translation.) As our propitiation, it was *reconciliation*, the making of peace for us with our

50

offended, estranged, angry Creator (Romans 5:9–11). We are not wise to play down God's hostility against us sinners; what we should do is magnify our Savior's achievement for us in displacing wrath by peace.

Again, as our reconciliation, the cross was *redemption*, rescue from bondage and misery by the payment of a price (see Ephesians 1:7; Romans 3:24; Revelation 5:9; Mark 10:45); and as redemption, it was *victory* over all hostile powers that had kept us, and wanted still to keep us, in sin and out of God's favor (Colossians 2:13–15). All these angles must be explored if we are to grasp the whole truth.

"The Son of God . . . loved me, and gave himself for me"; so "God forbid that I should glory, save in the cross of our Lord Jesus Christ" (Galatians 2:20; 6:14, KJV). So said Paul. Thank God, I can identify. Can you?

FURTHER BIBLE STUDY

The meaning of the cross: Isaiah 53
Romans 3:19–26
Hebrews 10:1–25

QUESTIONS FOR THOUGHT AND DISCUSSION

What is the full meaning which Christians find in the word "suffered" (Latin *passus*)?

"Both God and men were agents of Jesus' passion." Explain.

What does Christ's death have to do with your sins?

10

He Descended into Hell

Death has been called "the new obscenity," the nasty thing which no polite person nowadays will talk about in public. But death, even when unmentionable, remains inescapable. The one sure fact of life is that one day, with or without warning, quietly or painfully, it is going to stop. How will I, then, cope with death when my turn comes?

CHRISTIAN VICTORY

Christians hold that the Jesus of the Scriptures is alive,

and that those who know him as Savior, Lord, and Friend find in this knowledge a way through all life's problems, dying included. For "Christ leads me through no darker rooms/Than he went through before." Having tasted death himself, he can support us while we taste it, and carry us through the great change to share the life beyond death into which he himself has passed. Death without Christ is "the king of terrors," but death with Christ loses the "sting," the power to hurt, which it otherwise would have.

John Preston, the Puritan, knew this. When he lay dying, they asked him if he feared death, now it was so close. "No," whispered Preston; "I shall change my *place*, but I shall not change my *company*." As if to say: I shall leave my friends, but not my Friend, for he will never leave me.

This is victory—victory over death, and the fear it brings. And it is to point the way to this victory that the Creed, before announcing Jesus' resurrection, declares: "he descended into hell." Though this clause did not establish itself in the Creed till the fourth century, and is therefore not used by some churches, what it says is of very great importance, as we can now see.

HADES, NOT GEHENNA

The English is misleading, for "hell" has changed its sense since the English form of the Creed was fixed. Originally, "hell" meant the place of the departed as such, corresponding to the Greek *Hades* and the Hebrew *Sheol*. That is what it means here, where the Creed echoes Peter's statement that Psalm 16:10, "thou wilt not abandon my soul to *Hades*" (so RSV: AV has "hell"), was a prophecy fulfilled when Jesus rose (see Acts 2:27–31). But since the seventeenth century "hell" has been used to signify only the state of final retribution for the godless, for which the New Testament name is *Gehenna*.

What the Creed means, however, is that Jesus entered, not *Gehenna*, but *Hades*—that is, that he really died, and that it was from a genuine death, not a simulated one, that he rose.

Perhaps it should be said (though one shrinks from laboring something so obvious) that "descended" does *not* imply that the way from Palestine to Hades is down into the ground, any more than "rose" implies that Jesus returned to surface level up the equivalent of a mine shaft! The language of descent is used because Hades, being the place of the disembodied, is *lower* in worth and dignity than is life on earth, where body and soul are together and humanity is in that sense whole.

JESUS IN HADES

"Being put to death in the flesh but made alive in the spirit" (1 Peter 3:18), Jesus entered Hades, and Scripture tells us briefly what he did there.

First, by his presence he made Hades into Paradise (a place of pleasure) for the penitent thief (cf. Luke 23:43), and presumably for all others who died trusting him during his earthly ministry, just as he does now for the faithful departed (see Philippians 1:21–23; 2 Corinthians 5:6–8).

Second, he *perfected* the spirits of Old Testament believers (Hebrews 12:23; cf. 11:40), bringing them out of the gloom which Sheol, the "pit," had hitherto been for them (cf. Psalm 88:3–6, 10–12), into this same Paradise experience. This is the core of truth in Medieval fantasies of the "harrowing of hell."

Third, 1 Peter 3:19 tells us that he "made proclamation" (presumably, of his kingdom and appointment as the world's judge) to the imprisoned "spirits" who had rebelled in antediluvian times (presumably, the fallen angels of 2 Peter 2:4 ff., who are also the "sons of God" of Genesis 6:1–4). Some have based on this one text a hope that all humans who did not hear the gospel in this life, or who having heard it rejected it, will have it savingly preached to them in the life to come, but Peter's words do not provide the least warrant for the inference.

What makes Jesus' entry into Hades important for us is not, however, any of this, but simply the fact that now we can face death knowing that when it comes we shall not find ourselves alone. He has been there before us, and he will see us through.

FURTHER BIBLE STUDY

The Christian's attitude toward death:
Philippians 1:19–26
2 Corinthians 5:1–10
2 Timothy 4:6–18

QUESTIONS FOR THOUGHT AND DISCUSSION

Define and differentiate the biblical terms *Hades, Sheol, Gehenna.*

How do we know that Christ's experience of death was genuine? What is the importance of this fact?

What difference does it make whether we face death with Christ or without him?

11
The
Third Day

Suppose that Jesus, having died on the cross, had stayed dead. Suppose that, like Socrates or Confucius, he was now no more than a beautiful memory. Would it matter? We should still have his example and teaching; wouldn't they be enough?

JESUS' RISING IS CRUCIAL

Enough for what? Not for Christianity. Had Jesus not risen, but stayed dead, the bottom would drop out of Christianity, for four things would then be true.

First, to quote Paul, 1 Corinthians 15:17: "if Christ has not been raised, your faith is futile and you are still in your sins."

Second, there is then no hope of our rising either; we must expect to stay dead too.

Third, if Jesus Christ is not risen, then he is not reigning and will not return, and every single item in the Creed after "suffered and was buried" will have to be struck out.

Fourth, Christianity cannot be what the first Christians thought it was—fellowship with a living Lord who is identical with the Jesus of the Gospels. The Jesus of the Gospels can still be your hero, but he cannot be your Savior.

A FACT OF HISTORY

To show that it views Jesus' resurrection as fact of history, the Creed actually times it—"the third day," counting inclusively (the ancients' way) from the day when Jesus was "crucified under Pontius Pilate" in about A.D. 30. On that precise day, in Jerusalem, capital of Palestine, Jesus came alive and vacated a rock tomb, and death was conquered for all time.

Can we be sure it happened? The evidence is solid. The tomb was empty, and nobody could produce the body. For more than a month after, the disciples kept meeting Jesus alive, always unexpectedly, usually in groups (from two to 500). Hallucinations don't happen this way!

The disciples, for their part, were sure that the risen Christ was no fancy, and tirelessly proclaimed his rising in face of ridicule, persecution, and even death—a most effective way of scotching the malicious rumor that they stole Jesus' body (cf. Matthew 28:11-15).

The corporate experience of the Christian church over nineteen centuries chimes in with the belief that Jesus rose, for the risen Lord truly "walks with me and talks with me along life's narrow way," and communion with him belongs to the basic Christian awareness of reality.

No sense can be made of any of this evidence save by supposing that Jesus really rose.

Well might Prof. C. F. D. Moule issue his challenge: "If the coming into existence of the Nazarenes, a phenomenon undeniably attested in the New Testament, rips a great hole in the history, a hole of the size and shape of the resurrection, what does the secular historian propose to stop it up with?" The actual historical effect is inconceivable without the resurrection of Jesus as its objective historical cause.

FACING THE EVIDENCE

A Christian in public debate accused his skeptical opponent of having more faith than he—"for," he said, "in face of the evidence, I can't believe that Jesus did not rise, and he can!" It really is harder to disbelieve the resurrection than to accept it, much harder. Have you yet seen it that way? To believe in Jesus Christ as Son of God and living Savior, and to echo the words of ex-doubter Thomas, "My Lord and my God," is certainly more than an exercise of reason, but in face of the evidence it is the only *reasonable* thing a man can do.

WHAT JESUS' RISING MEANS

What is the significance of Jesus' rising? In a word, it marked Jesus out as Son of God (Romans 1:4); it vindicated his righteousness (John 16:10); it demonstrated victory over death (Acts 2:24); it guaranteed the believer's forgiveness and justification (1 Corinthians 15:17; Romans 4:25), and his own future resurrection too (1 Corinthians 15:18); and it brings him into the reality of resurrection life now (Romans 6:4). Marvelous! You could speak of Jesus' rising as the most hopeful—hope-full—thing that has ever happened—and you would be right!

FURTHER BIBLE STUDY

The resurrection of Jesus: John 20:1–18
1 Corinthians 15:1–28

QUESTIONS FOR THOUGHT AND DISCUSSION

How would Christianity be different if Christ had not risen?

What evidence is there for Jesus' resurrection?

Why does Packer speak of believing that Christ rose as "the only reasonable thing a man can do"? Do you agree?

12
He Ascended into Heaven

"He ascended" echoes Jesus' "I ascend" (John 20:17; compare 6:62). "Into heaven" echoes "taken up from you into heaven," the angels' words in the Ascension story (Acts 1:10). But what is "heaven"? Is it the sky, or outer space? Does the Creed mean that Jesus was the first astronaut? No, both it and the Bible are making a different point.

WHAT HEAVEN MEANS

"Heaven" in the Bible means three things: 1. The endless, self-sustaining life of God. In this sense, God always dwelt "in heaven," even when there was no earth. 2. The state of angels or men as they share the life of God, whether in foretaste now or in fullness hereafter. In this sense, the Christian's reward, treasure, and inheritance are all "in heaven" and heaven is shorthand for the Christian's final hope. 3. The sky, which, being above us and more like infinity than anything else we know, is an emblem in space and time of God's eternal life, just as the rainbow is an emblem of his everlasting covenant (see Genesis 9:8–17).

Bible and Creed proclaim that in the Ascension, forty days after his rising, Jesus entered heaven in sense 2 in a new and momentous way: thenceforth he "sitteth on the right hand of God the Father almighty," ruling all things in his Father's name and with his Father's almightiness for the long-term good of his people. "On the right hand of God" signifies not a palatial location but a regal function: see Acts 2:33ff.; Romans 8:34; Ephesians 1:20ff.; Hebrews 1:3, 13; 10:12ff.; 12:2. He "ascended far above the heavens" (that is, reentered his pre-incarnate life, a life unrestricted by anything created) "that he might fill all things" (that is, make his kingly power effective everywhere; see Ephesians 4:10). "Ascended" is, of course, a picture-word implying exaltation ("going up!") to a condition of supreme dignity and power.

THE ASCENSION

What happened at the Ascension, then, was not that Jesus became a spaceman, but that his disciples were shown a *sign*, just as at the Transfiguration. As C. S. Lewis puts it, "they saw first a short vertical movement and then a vague luminosity (that is what 'cloud' presumably means . . .) and then nothing." In other words, Jesus' final withdrawal from human sight, to rule till he returns to judgment, was presented to the disciples' outward eyes as a going up into heaven in sense 3. This should not puzzle us. Withdrawal had to take place somehow, and going up, down, or sideways, failing to appear or suddenly vanishing were the only possible ways. Which would signify most clearly that Jesus would henceforth be reigning in glory? That answers itself.

So the message of the Ascension story is: "Jesus the Savior reigns!"

OUR HEARTS IN HEAVEN

In a weary world in which grave philosophers were counseling suicide as man's best option, the unshakeable, rollicking optimism of the first Christians, who went on feeling on top of the world however much the world seemed to be on top of them, made a vast impression. (It still does, when Christians are Christian enough to show it!) Three certainties were, and are, its secret.

The first concerns God's *world*. It is that Christ really rules it, that he has won a decisive victory over the dark powers that had mastered it, and that the manifesting of this fact is only a matter of time. God's war with Satan is now like a chess game in which the result is sure but the losing player has not yet given up, or like the last phase of human hostilities in which the defeated enemy's counterattacks, though fierce and frequent, cannot succeed, and are embraced in the victor's strategy as mere mopping-up operations. One wishes that our reckoning of dates "A.D." (*anno Domini*, in the year of our Lord), which starts in intention (though probably a few years too late) with Jesus' birth, had been calculated from the year of the cross, resurrection, and ascension; for that was when Jesus' Lordship became the cosmic fact that it is today.

The second certainty concerns God's *Christ*. It is that our reigning Lord "intercedes" for us (Romans 8:34; Hebrews 7:25), in the sense that he appears "in the presence of God" as our "advocate" (Hebrews 9:24; 1 John 2:1)

62

to ensure that we receive "grace to help" in our need (Hebrews 4:16) and so are kept to the end in the love of God (cf. the Good Shepherd's pledge, John 10:27–29). "Intercede" denotes, not a suppliant making an appeal to charity, but the intervening of one who has sovereign right and power to make requests and take action in another's interest. It is truly said that our Lord's presence and life in heaven as the enthroned priest-king, our propitiation, so to speak, in person, is itself his intercession: just for him to be there guarantees all grace to us, and glory too.

An eighteenth-century jingle puts this certainty into words which make the heart leap:

> *Love moved thee to die;*
> *And on this I rely,*
> *My Saviour hath loved me, I cannot tell why:*
> *But this I can find,*
> *We two are so joined*
> *He'll not be in glory and leave me behind.*

The third certainty concerns God's *people*. It is a matter of God-given experience, as well as of God-taught understanding. It is that Christians enjoy here and now a hidden life of fellowship with the Father and the Son which nothing, not even death itself, can touch—for it is the life of the world to come begun already, the life of heaven tasted here on earth. The explanation of this experience, which all God's people know in some measure, is that believers have actually passed through death (not as a physical, but as a personal and psychic, event) into the eternal life which lies beyond. "You have died, and your life is hid with Christ in God" (Colossians 3:3; cf. 2:12; Romans 6:3, 4). "God . . . when we were dead . . . made us alive together with Christ . . . and raised us up with him, and made us sit with him in the heavenly places in Christ Jesus" (Ephesians 2:4ff.).

The Prayer Book collect for Ascension Day prays God to "grant . . . that like as we do believe thy only-begotten Son our Lord Jesus Christ to have ascended into heavens; so we may also in heart and mind thither ascend, and with him continually dwell." May we be enabled, in the power of these three certainties, to do just that.

FURTHER BIBLE STUDY

The significance of the Ascension: Acts 1:1–11
Ephesians 1:15—
2:10

QUESTIONS FOR THOUGHT AND DISCUSSION

In what sense did Jesus ascend to heaven?
To what did he return?
What is Christ doing now? What importance has this heavenly ministry for us?

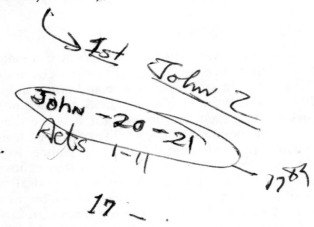

13
He
Shall Come

The core of the Creed is its witness to the past, present, and future of Jesus Christ: his birth, death, rising, and ascension in the past; his reign now; and his coming at a future date to judge. ("Quick" in "the quick and the dead," by the way, means living, not fast-moving.) With his coming, Scripture tells us, will come our bodily resurrection and the full everlasting life of which the Creed speaks. A new cosmic order will start then too. *There's a great day coming.* (See Matthew 25:14–46; John 5:25–29; Romans

8:18–24; 2 Peter 3:10–13; Revelation 20:11—21:4.)

THE CHRISTIAN'S HOPE

Nowhere does the strength of the Creed as a charter for life come out more clearly. In today's world, pessimism prevails because people lack hope. They foresee only the bomb, or bankruptcy, or a weary old age—nothing worthwhile. Communists and Jehovah's Witnesses attract by offering bright hopes of heaven on earth—following the Revolution in one case, Armageddon in the other; but Christians have a hope that outshines both—the hope of which Bunyan's Mr. Stand-fast said, "the thoughts of what I am going to . . . lie as a glowing Coal at my Heart." The Creed highlights this hope when it declares: "he shall come."

In one sense, Christ comes for every Christian at death, but the Creed looks to the day when he will come publicly to wind up history and judge all men—Christians as Christians, accepted already, whom a "blood-bought free reward" awaits according to the faithfulness of their service; rebels as rebels, to be rejected by the Master whom they rejected first. The judgments of Jesus, "the righteous judge" (2 Timothy 4:8; compare Romans 2:5–11), will raise no moral problems.

CERTAIN AND GLORIOUS

Some think it will never happen—but we have God's word for it, and sober scientists now tell us that an end to our world through nuclear or ecological catastrophe is a real possibility. Christ's coming is unimaginable—but man's imagination is no measure of God's power, and the Jesus who is spiritually present to millions simultaneously now can surely make himself visibly present to the risen race then. We do not know when he will come (so we must always be ready), nor how he will come (why not in the going off of a bomb?)—but "we know that when he appears we shall be like him, for we shall see him as he is" (1 John 3:2)—and that is knowledge enough! "Come, Lord Jesus" (Revelation 22:20).

ECLIPSED

The hope of Christ's return thrilled the New Testament Christians, as witness over 300 references to it in the documents—on average, one every thirteen verses. But to us it is not so much exciting as embarrassing! The phrase "Cinderella of the Creed," which was once applied to the Holy Spirit, nowadays fits Christ's return much more truly. Why is it thus in eclipse? For four main reasons, it seems.

First, this is a time of *reaction* from a century and a half of intense prophetic study expressing a spirit of prayerless pessimism about the church and doom-watching detachment from the world. This spirit, and the dogmatism that went with it about both the signs and the date of Christ's coming (despite Mark 13:32 and Acts 1:7!), were quite unjustifiable, and have given the topic a bad name.

Second, this is a time of *skepticism* as to whether Christ personally and physically rose and ascended, and this naturally spawns dithering doubts as to whether we can hope ever to see him again.

Third, this is a time of *timidity,* in which Christians while querying the materialistic self-sufficiency of Western secularism and Marxist ideologies hesitate to challenge their "this-worldly" preoccupation, lest the counter-accusation be provoked that Christians do not care about social and economic justice. So the fact that Christ will end this world, and that the best part of the Christian hope lies beyond it, gets played down.

Fourth, this is a time of *worldly-mindedness,* at least among the prosperous Christians of the West. We think less and less about the better things that Christ will bring us at his reappearance, because our thoughts are increasingly absorbed by the good things we enjoy here. No one would wish persecution or destitution on another, but who can deny that at this point they might do us good?

All four attitudes are unhealthy and unworthy. God help us to transcend them.

BE PREPARED

"Be ready," said the Savior to his disciples, "for the Son of man is coming at an hour you do not expect" (Matthew 24:44). How does one get and stay ready? By keeping short accounts with God and men; by taking life a day at a time, as Jesus told us to do (Matthew 6:34); and by heeding the advice of Bishop Ken's hymn, "Live each day as if thy last." Budget and plan for an ordinary span of years, but in spirit be packed up and ready to leave at any time. This should be part of our daily devotional discipline. When the Lord comes, he should find his people praying for revival and planning world evangelism—but packed up and ready to leave nonetheless. If Boy Scouts can learn to live realistically in terms of the motto "Be prepared" for any ordinary thing that might happen, why are Christians so slow to learn the same lesson in relation to the momentous event of Christ's return?

FURTHER BIBLE STUDY

The Christian's attitude toward Christ's return:
Luke 12:35–48
1 Thessalonians 4:13—5:11
2 Peter 3

QUESTIONS FOR THOUGHT AND DISCUSSION

In what way is Christ's future coming reason for hope?

When Christ returns, what will he do? What are your reactions to knowing this?

What does the Bible not tell us about Christ's return? Why do you think God withholds this information?

Gen. 1:2
        2:26
Exodus 3 1-6
Judges 13:25
Mathew 1:20
John 7 37-39
Romans (8) 9-10
John CH 16 vs 4-15   Study

14

I Believe in the Holy Ghost

Originally, "ghost" meant the unit of psychic energy in a man, and belief in ghosts (in the modern sense) reflects the belief that this personal energy may still act when disembodied. With this meaning, "ghost" was a good word for "spirit" in the Bible, for the Hebrew and Greek words (*ruach, pneuma*), from meaning wind, had both come to signify personal energy, human and divine. But when, as now, "ghost" suggests something frightening and nasty, it is better to call the third divine Person the Holy *Spirit*.

"I believe in the Holy Spirit": so starts the Creed's third paragraph. From the creating work of the Father and the rescue work of the Son, it turns to the re-creating work of the Spirit, whereby men are actually made new in and through Christ. So we hear of *church* (new community), *forgiveness* (new relationship), *resurrection* (new existence), and *everlasting life* (new fulfillment). But first comes a profession of faith in the Spirit himself.

THE SPIRIT OF CHRIST

He is divine ("holy" says this). He is an active Person, the Executive of the Godhead. Yes, but doing and aiming at what? Misbelief abounds here. Some associate the Spirit with mystical states and artistic inspirations, both Christian and pagan. Others link the Spirit only with unusual Christian experiences—feeling "high" (to use the world's word), seeking visions, receiving revelations, speaking in tongues, healing. But these are secondary elements of the Spirit's work, where they derive from the Spirit at all.

The Old Testament mentions the Spirit in connection with creation, both divine (Genesis 1:2) and human (Exodus 31:1–6); the inspiring of God's spokesmen (Isaiah 61:1; the Nicene Creed states that the Spirit "spoke by the prophets"); the equipping and enabling of God's servants (judges, kings, etc.; e.g., Judges 13:25; 14:19; Isaiah 11:2; Zechariah 4:6); and the evoking of godliness in individuals and in the community (Psalm 51:11; Ezekiel 36:26ff.; 37:1–14; Zechariah 12:10). All this gains deeper meaning in the New Testament, where the Spirit is shown to be a personal agent distinct from the Father and the Son, and is spoken of as the Spirit of Christ (Romans 8:9; 1 Peter 1:11).

The key to understanding the New Testament view of the Spirit's work is to see that his purpose is identical with the Father's—namely, to see glory and praise come to the Son. Accordingly—

First, the Spirit serviced the Son throughout his earthly life from the moment when, as the Creed says, he was "conceived by the Holy Ghost" (Matthew 1:20). The Spirit's dove-like descent on him at his baptism showed not only that he was the Spirit-giver, but also that he was himself Spirit-filled (Luke 4:1; cf. verses 14, 18). It was "through the eternal Spirit" that he offered himself in sacrifice for us (Hebrews 9:14).

Second, the Spirit now acts as Jesus' agent—"another Comforter" (helper, supporter, advocate, encourager). He shows Jesus to us through the gospel, unites us to him by faith, and indwells us to change us "into his likeness" by causing "the fruit of the Spirit" to grow in us (2 Corinthians 3:18; Galatians 5:22ff.).

"He will glorify [not himself but] me, for he will take what is mine and declare it to you" (John 16:14). Jesus' words indicate the self-effacing character of the Spirit; he functions as a floodlight trained on Christ, so that it is Christ, not the Spirit, whom we see. In the gospel message, Jesus is set before us throughout, saying: Come to me; follow me. In our conscience as we hear the gospel with the inner ear of faith, the Spirit, standing behind us as it were to throw light over our shoulder on to Jesus, constantly urges: Go to him; deal with him. So we do—and it is this that makes our life Christian.

WITNESS AND MINISTRY

The Spirit is *witness* and *teacher* (1 John 5:7; 2:27; cf. 4:2ff.) inasmuch as, first, he convinces us that the Jesus of the gospel, the New Testament Christ, really exists, and is what he is "for us men, and for our salvation"; second, he assures us that as believers we are God's children and heirs with Christ (Romans 8:16ff.); third, he moves us to bear witness to the Christ whom his witness led us to know (cf. John 15:26). What the Spirit's witnessing effects is not private revelation of something hitherto undisclosed, but personal reception of God's public testimony which was "there" all along in the Scriptures, but went unheeded. Paul is describing the Spirit's work of witness when he speaks of "having the eyes of your hearts enlightened" (Ephesians 1:18).

Third, the Spirit gives to every Christian one or more gifts (i.e., capacities to express Christ in serving God and man), so that "every-member ministry" in the church, which is Christ's body, may become a reality (1 Corinthians 12:4–7; Ephesians 4:11–16). This manifold ministry is itself Christ's own ministry continuing from heaven, through us as his hands, feet, and mouth; and the Spirit's bestowing of gifts should be seen as further servicing and glorifying of Christ on his part, inasmuch as it is the means whereby Christ's personal ministry to men is able to go on.

SIGNS OF THE SPIRIT

What then are the signs that Christ's self-effacing Spirit is at work? Not mystical raptures, nor visions and supposed revelations, nor even healings, tongues, and apparent miracles; for Satan, playing on our psychosomatic complexity and our fallenness, can produce all these things (cf. 2 Thessalonians 2:9ff.; Colossians 2:18). The only sure signs are that the Christ of the Bible is acknowledged, trusted, loved for his grace and served for his glory, and that believers actually turn from sin to the life of holiness which is Christ's image in his people (cf. 1 Corinthians 12:3; 2 Corinthians 3:17). These are the criteria by which we must judge, for instance, the modern "charismatic renewal," and Christian Science (reaching, perhaps, different verdicts in the two cases).

So when I say, as a Christian, "I believe in the Holy Ghost," my meaning should be, first, that I believe personal fellowship, across space and time, with the living Christ of the New Testament to be a reality, which through the Spirit I have found; second, that I am open to be led by the Spirit, who now indwells me, into Christian knowledge, obedience, and service, and I expect to be so led each day; and, third, that I bless him as the author of my assurance that I am a son and heir of God. Truly, it is a glorious thing to believe in the Holy Spirit!

FURTHER BIBLE STUDY

The Spirit's ministry: John 7:37–39; 14:15–26; 16:7–15
Romans 8:1–17

QUESTIONS FOR THOUGHT AND DISCUSSION

How does the work of the Spirit differ from that of the Father and the Son?

What does the Holy Spirit do as "Jesus' agent"?

What would you say to a professed Christian who doubted if he had ever experienced the ministry of the Holy Spirit?

15
The Holy
Catholic Church

It is by strict theological logic that the Creed confesses faith in the Holy Spirit before proceeding to the church, and that it speaks of the church before mentioning personal salvation (forgiveness, resurrection, everlasting life). For though Father and Son have loved the church and the Son has redeemed it, it is the Holy Spirit who actually creates it, by inducing faith; and it is in the church, through its ministry and fellowship, that personal salvation ordinarily comes to be enjoyed.

Unhappily, there is at this point a parting of the ways. Roman Catholics and Protestants both say the Creed, yet they are divided. Why? Basically, because of divergent understandings of "I believe in the holy catholic church"—"one holy catholic and apostolic church," as the true text of the Nicene Creed has it.

ROMAN VERSUS PROTESTANT

Official Roman Catholic teaching presents the church of Christ as the *one* organized body of baptized persons who are in communion with the Pope and acknowledge the teaching and ruling authority of the episcopal hierarchy. It is *holy* because it produces saintly men and is kept from radical sin; *catholic* because in its worldwide spread it holds the full faith in trust for all men; and *apostolic* because its ministerial orders stem from the apostles, and its faith (including such nonbiblical items as the assumption of Mary and her immaculate conception, the Mass-sacrifice, and papal infallibility) is a sound growth from apostolic roots. Non-Roman bodies, however church-like, are not strictly part of the church at all.

Protestants challenge this from the Bible. In Scripture (they say) the church is the *one* worldwide fellowship of believing people whose Head is Christ. It is *holy* because it is consecrated to God (though it is capable nonetheless of grievous sin); it is *catholic* because it embraces all Christians everywhere; and it is *apostolic* because it seeks to maintain the apostles' doctrine unmixed. Pope, hierarchy, and extra-biblical doctrines are not merely nonessential but actually deforming; if Rome is a church (which some Reformers doubted) she is so despite the extras, not because of them. In particular, infallibility belongs to God speaking in the Bible, not to the church nor to any of its officers, and any teaching given in or by the church must be open to correction by what Anglican Article XX calls "God's word written."

Some Protestants have taken the clause "the communion of saints" which follows "the holy catholic church" as the Creed's own elucidation of what the church is; namely, Christians in fellowship with each other—just that, without regard for any particular hierarchical structure. But it is usual to treat this phrase as affirming the real union in Christ of the church "militant here in earth" with the church triumphant, as is indicated in Hebrews 12:22–24; and it may be that the clause was originally meant to signify *communion in holy things* (word, sacrament, worship, prayers), and to make the true but distinct point that in the church there is a real sharing in the life of God. The "spiritual" view of the church as being a fellowship before it is an institution can, however, be confirmed from Scripture without appeal to this phrase, whatever its sense, being needed.

THE NEW TESTAMENT

That the New Testament presents the Protestant view is hardly open to dispute (the dispute is over whether the New Testament is final!). The church appears in trinitarian relationships, as the family of God the Father, the body of Christ the Son, and the temple (dwelling-place) of the Holy Spirit, and so long as the dominical sacraments are administered and ministerial oversight is exercised, no organizational norms are insisted on at all. The church is the supernatural society of God's redeemed and baptized people, looking back to Christ's first coming with gratitude and on to his second coming with hope. "Your life is hid with Christ in God. When Christ who is our life appears, then you also will appear with him in glory" (Colossians 3:3ff.)—such is the church's present state and future prospect. To this hope both sacraments point, baptism prefiguring final resurrection, the Lord's Supper anticipating "the marriage supper of the Lamb" (Revelation 19:9).

For the present, however, all churches (like those in Corinth, Colossae, Galatia, and Thessalonica, to look no fur-

76

ther) are prone to err in both faith and morals, and need constant correction and re-formation at all levels (intellectual, devotional, structural, liturgical) by the Spirit through God's Word.

The evangelical theology of revival, first spelled out in the seventeenth and eighteenth centuries, and the present-day emergence of "charismatic renewal" on a worldwide scale, reminds us of something which Roman Catholic and Protestant disputers, in their concentration on doctrinal truth, tended to miss—namely, that churches must always be open to the immediacy of the Spirit's Lordship, and that disorderly vigor in a congregation is infinitely preferable to a correct and tidy deadness.

THE LOCAL CHURCH

The acid test of the church's state is what happens in the local congregation. Each congregation is a visible outcrop of the one church universal, called to serve God and men in humility and, perhaps, humiliation while living in prospect of glory. Spirit-filled for worship and witness, active in love and care for insiders and outsiders alike, self-supporting and self-propagating, each congregation is to be a spearhead of divine counterattack for the recapture of a rebel world.

Tailpiece: how is your congregation getting on?

FURTHER BIBLE STUDY

The church's nature and destiny: 1 Peter 2
Ephesians 2:11—
4:16

QUESTIONS FOR THOUGHT AND DISCUSSION

How does the Roman Catholic use of the New Testament differ from the Protestant one? How does this affect the concept each holds of the church?

77

How does Packer define "the communion of saints"?
Do you agree with what he says? Why or why not?

What is the function of a local Christian church in relation to the universal church?

16
Forgiveness of Sins

What are sins? Sin, says the Westminster Shorter Catechism, is "any want of conformity unto, or transgression
of, the law of God." This echoes 1 John 3:4, "sin is lawlessness." It has other aspects too. It is lawlessness in relation
to God as lawgiver, rebellion in relation to God as rightful
ruler, missing the mark in relation to God as our designer,
guilt in relation to God as judge, and uncleanness in relation to God as the Holy One.

Sin is a perversity touching each one of us at every point

in our lives. Apart from Jesus Christ, no human being has ever been free of its infection. It appears in desires as well as deeds, and motives as well as actions. Rightly does the Anglican Prayer Book teach us to say, "We have followed too much the devices and desires of our own hearts. . . . We have left undone those things which we ought to have done, and we have done those things which we ought not to have done, and (spiritually) there is no health in us."

Sin is everybody's problem in the sight of God. for he is "of purer eyes than to behold evil," and cannot *"look on wrong"* (Habakkuk 1:13). But we find life to be a moral minefield for us; and the harder we try to avoid sin the more often we find—too late—that we have stepped where we shouldn't, and been blown to pieces so far as the required love of God and our neighbor is concerned. And where does that leave us?—"for the wrath of God is revealed from heaven against all ungodliness and wickedness of men" (Romans 1:18).

The good news, however, is this—sins can be forgiven. Central to the gospel is the glorious "but" of Psalm 130:4—"If thou, O Lord, shouldst mark iniquities, Lord, who could stand? *But* there is forgiveness with thee, that thou mayest be feared"—that is, worshiped with loyalty (for that is what *fear* of God means).

VITAL AND REAL

Forgiveness is pardon in a personal setting. It is taking back into friendship those who went against you, hurt you, and put themselves in the wrong with you. It is *compassionate* (showing unmerited kindness to the wrongdoer), *creative* (renewing the spoiled relationship)—and, inevitably, *costly.* God's forgiveness is the supreme instance of this, for it is God in love restoring fellowship at the cost of the cross.

If our sins were unforgivable, where should we be? A

bad conscience is the most universal experience—and the most wretched. No outward change relieves it; you carry it with you all your waking hours. The more conscientious you are, the more your knowledge of having failed others, and God too, will haunt you. Without forgiveness you will have no peace. A bad conscience delivering at full strength, tearing you to pieces in the name of God, is hell indeed, both here and hereafter.

LUTHER KNEW IT

A man distressed about sin wrote to Luther. The Reformer, who himself had suffered long agonies over this problem, replied: "Learn to know Christ and him crucified. Learn to sing to him and say—Lord Jesus, you are my righteousness, I am your sin. You took on you what was mine; you set on me what was yours. You became what you were not that I might become what I was not." Compare Paul: "For our sake [God] made [Christ] to be sin who knew no sin, so that in him we might become the righteousness of God" (2 Corinthians 5:21). Link up with Jesus, the living Lord, by faith, and the great exchange is fulfilled. Through Jesus' atoning death God accepts you as righteous, and cancels your sins. This is justification, forgiveness, and peace.

Paul in Romans and Galatians, and the Reformers after him, spoke of justification rather than of forgiveness. This is because justification is forgiveness *plus;* it signifies not only a washing out of the past, but also acceptance and the gift of a righteous man's status for the future. Also, justification is final, being a decision on which God will never go back, and so it is the basis of assurance, whereas present forgiveness does not necessarily argue more than temporary forbearance. So justification—public acquittal and reinstatement before God's judgment-seat—is actually the richer concept.

BY FAITH ONLY

In the past (things are less clear-cut today) Roman Catholics did not grasp the decisiveness of present justification, nor see that Christ's righteousness ("my Savior's obedience and blood," as Toplady put it) is its whole ground, nor realize that our part is to stop trying to earn it, and simply take it as God's free gift of grace. So they insisted that sacraments, "good works," and purgatorial pains hereafter were all necessary means of final acceptance, because they were among the grounds on which that acceptance was based. But the Reformers preached, as Paul did, full and final acceptance through a decisive act of forgiveness here and now; this, they said, is by faith only.

Why faith *only?* Because Christ's righteousness *only* is the basis of pardon and peace, and Christ and his gifts are received *only* by faith's embrace. Faith means not only believing God's truth, but trusting Christ, taking what he offers, and then triumphing in the knowledge of what is now yours.

Is God's gift of forgiveness by faith yours yet? It is easily missed. The Jews missed it, said Paul; their tragedy was that their zeal for God led them to try to establish their own righteousness (i.e., earn his acceptance), and "they did not submit to God's righteousness" (i.e., to his way of forgiving and justifying, by faith in Christ only): see Romans 10:2ff. The pathetic truth is that we sinners are self-righteous to the core, and we are constantly justifying ourselves, and we hate admitting that there is anything seriously wrong with us, anything that God or man might seriously hold against us; and we have to do violence to our own perverted instincts at this point before faith is possible for us. God save us all from repeating the tragedy of the Jews in our own lives.

FURTHER BIBLE STUDY

Justification through Christ by faith apart from works:

Romans 5; 10:1–13
Galatians 2:15—3:29
Philippians 3:4–16

QUESTIONS FOR THOUGHT AND DISCUSSION

What is forgiveness, and what does it do for the forgiven on a personal level?

What did Luther mean by saying, "You became what you were not that I might become what I was not"?

Why is it that forgiveness comes through faith *only?*

17
Resurrection of the Body

Scripture sees death—life's one certainty—not as a friend but as a destroyer. When my body and soul separate, I shall only be a shadow of what I was. My body is part of me, the apparatus of my self-expression; without it, all my power to make things, do things, and relate to my fellows is gone. Think of someone with full use of his faculties, and compare him with a paralytic; now compare the paralytic with someone totally disembodied, and you will see what I mean. Paralytics can do little enough; disembodied persons, less still. Thus death, while not ending our existence, nullifies and in a real sense destroys it.

COPING WITH DEATH

Death is the fundamental human problem, for if death is really final nothing is worthwhile save self-indulgence. "If the dead are not raised, let us eat and drink, for tomorrow we die" (1 Corinthians 15:32). And no philosophy or religion which cannot come to terms with death is any real use to us.

Here, however, Christianity stands out. Alone among the world's faiths and "isms" it views death as conquered. For Christian faith is hope resting on fact—namely, the fact that Jesus rose bodily from the grave and now lives eternally in heaven. The hope is that when Jesus comes back—the day when history stops and this world ends— he will "change our lowly body to be like his glorious body" (Philippians 3:21; cf. 1 John 3:2). This hope embraces all who have died in Christ as well as Christians alive at his appearing: "for the hour is coming when all who are in the tombs will hear [Jesus'] voice and come forth, those who have done good, to the resurrection of life" (John 5:28ff.). And the raising of the *body* means the restoring of the *person*—not just part of me, but all of me— to active, creative, undying life, for God and with God.

NEW BODY

In raising believers, God completes their redemption by the gift, not of their old bodies somehow patched up, but of new bodies fit for new men. Through regeneration and sanctification God has already renewed them inwardly; now they receive bodies to match. The new body is linked with the old, yet different from it, just as plants are linked with, yet different from, the seeds from which they grew (see 1 Corinthians 15:35–44). My present body—"brother ass," as Francis of Assisi would have me call it—is like a student's old jalopy; care for it as I will, it goes precariously and never very well, and often lets me and my Master down (very frustrating!). But my new body will feel and behave like a Rolls-Royce, and then my service will no longer be spoiled.

No doubt, like me, you both love your body because it is part of you and get mad at the way it limits you. So we should. And it is good to know that God's aim in giving us second-rate physical frames here is to prepare us for managing better bodies hereafter. As C. S. Lewis says somewhere, they give you unimpressive horses to learn to ride on, and only when you are ready for it are you allowed an animal that will gallop and jump.

A dwarf I knew would weep for joy at the thought of the body God had in store for him on resurrection day, and when I think of other Christians known to me who in one way or another are physical wrecks—deformed, decaying, crippled, hormonally unbalanced, or otherwise handicapped—I can weep too for this particular element of joy which will be theirs—and yours—and mine when that day dawns.

SOUL AND BODY

This bit of the Creed was probably put in to ward off the idea (very common for three centuries after Christ, and not unknown today) that man's hope is immortality for his soul, which (so it was thought) would be much better off disembodied. There was a tag, "the body is a tomb," which summed up this view. But it shows a wrong view both of matter (which God made, and likes, and declares good) and of man (who is not a noble soul able to excuse the shameful things he does by blaming them on to his uncouth material shell, but a psycho-physical unit whose moral state is directly expressed by his physical behavior). The disordering effect of sin is very clear in the way my physical appetites function (not to look further); but for all that these appetites are part of me and I must acknowledge moral responsibility for whatever active expression they find. The Bible doctrine of judgment is that each of us receives "good or evil, according to what he has done in the body" (2 Corinthians 5:10).

LIKE CHRIST

The promise that one day we shall have bodies "like his glorious body" (Philippians 3:20ff.) challenges us—do we really, from our hearts, welcome and embrace our promised destiny of being like Christ? (Cf. 1 John 3:2ff.) Facing this question could be a moment of truth for us. For some find their whole identity in gratifying physical itches (for sexual excitement, sleep, food, exercise, violence, alcoholic or drug-induced "highs," or whatever) and feel—alas, with too much truth—that were they deprived of these nothing would be left of them but an ache; and they see Jesus, who was not led by physical itches, as the "pale Galilean" through whose breath, according to Swinburne, the world grew cold, and whom D. H. Lawrence wanted to humanize (I have to use that verb in fairness to Lawrence, though it is the wackiest nonsense I have ever written) by imagining for him a sex life with a pagan priestess. Such a vision makes the idea of being like Jesus—that, and no more—sound like being sentenced to a living death. Now is that how, deep down, it sounds to you?

If so, only one thing can be said. Ask God to show you how Jesus' life, body and soul, was the only fully human life that has ever been lived, and keep looking at Jesus, as you meet him in the Gospels, till you can see it. Then the prospect of being like him—that, and no less—will seem to you the noblest and most magnificent destiny possible, and by embracing it you will become a true disciple. But until you see it—please believe me: I kid you not—there is no hope for you at all.

87

FURTHER BIBLE STUDY

The resurrection hope: Mark 12:18–27
1 Corinthians 15:35–58
Philippians 3:4–16

QUESTIONS FOR THOUGHT AND DISCUSSION

Why is a religion that does not deal with death valueless to us?

What evidence does the Bible give to show that death has been conquered?

How much can we say that we know about the state of the resurrected?

18
The Life Everlasting

Skeptics like Fred Hoyle and the late Bertrand Russell have told us that the thought of an endless future life horrifies them; for (they said) it would be so boring! Evidently they have found this life boring, and cannot imagine how human existence could be made permanently interesting and worthwhile. Poor fellows! Here we see the blighting effects of godlessness, and the black pessimism to which it leads.

But not all moderns are like Hoyle and Russell. Some

are anxious to survive death. Hence their interest in spiritist phenomena, supposed to give proof of survival. But three facts should be noted. First, "messages" from the departed are distressingly trivial and self-absorbed. Second, "messages" do not come from those who in this life walked close to God. Third, mediums and their "controls" are embarrassed by the name of Jesus. These facts give warning that spiritist phenomena, whatever their true explanation, are a blind alley for investigating "the blessed hope of everlasting life."

JESUS' PRESENCE MAKES HEAVEN

When the Creed speaks of "*the* life everlasting" it means, not just endless existence (demons and lost souls have that), but the final joy into which Jesus entered (Hebrews 12:2), and which he promised and prayed that his followers would one day share. "Where I am, there shall my servant be also; if any one serves me, the Father will honor him. Father, I desire that they also, whom thou hast given me, may be with me where I am, to behold my glory" (John 12:26; 17:24).

Being with Jesus is the essence of heaven; it is what the life everlasting is all about. "I have formerly lived by hearsay and faith," said Bunyan's Mr. Stand-fast, "but now I go where I shall live by sight, and shall be with him, in whose company I delight myself." What shall we do in heaven? Not lounge around!—but worship, work, think, and communicate, enjoying activity, beauty, people, and God. First and foremost, however, we shall see and love Jesus, our Savior, Master, and Friend.

ENDLESS JOY

The everlastingness of this life was spelled out in the vividest possible way by the anonymous benefactor who appended to John Newton's "Amazing Grace" this extra verse:

90

> *When we've been there ten thousand years,*
> *Bright shining as the sun,*
> *We've no less days to sing God's praise*
> *Than when we first begun.*

I have been writing with enthusiasm, for this everlasting life is something to which I look forward. Why? Not because I am out of love with life here—just the reverse! My life is full of joy, from four sources—knowing God, and people, and the good and pleasant things that God and men under God have created, and doing things which are worthwhile for God or others, or for myself as God's man. But my reach exceeds my grasp. My relationships with God and men are never as rich and full as I want them to be, and I am always finding more than I thought was there in great music, great verse, great books, great lives, and the great kaleidoscope of the natural order. Jelly-Roll Morton sang of jazz, "The more I have, the more I want, it seems"—and there are 1,001 things (including Morton's own jazz) about which I find myself saying just that.

As I get older, I find that I appreciate God, and people, and good and lovely and noble things, more and more intensely; so it is pure delight to think that this enjoyment will continue and increase in some form (what form, God knows, and I am content to wait and see), literally forever. Christians inherit in fact the destiny which fairy tales envisaged in fancy: *we* (yes, you and I, the silly saved sinners) *live,* and live *happily,* and by God's endless mercy will live happily *ever after.*

We cannot visualize heaven's life, and the wise man will not try. Instead, he will dwell on the doctrine of heaven, which is that there the redeemed find all their heart's desire: joy with their Lord, joy with his people, and joy in the ending of all frustration and distress and the supply of all wants. What was said to the child—"If you want

91

sweets and hamsters in heaven, they'll be there"—was not an evasion, but a witness to the truth that in heaven no felt needs or longings go unsatisfied. What our wants will actually be, however, we hardly know, save that first and foremost we shall want to be "always . . . with the Lord" (1 Thessalonians 4:17).

Often now we say in moments of great enjoyment, "I don't want this ever to stop"—but it does. Heaven, however, is different. May heaven's joys be yours, and mine.

FURTHER BIBLE STUDY

Our destination: Revelation 21:1—22:5

QUESTIONS FOR THOUGHT AND DISCUSSION

Why is Packer suspicious of spiritist phenomena?

Why will heaven be delightful? Do you personally expect and look forward to heaven? Why or why not?

What will the residents of heaven do?